I need more than luck to remember my passwords!

Kay D Johnson

Johnson, Kay D
I Need More Than Luck To Remember My Passwords!

ISBN 978-1792167157(pkb)

Since this book holds all your private and valuable information, please keep this book in a safe place at all times.

A

Website:
Email:
User Name:
Password:
Security Question/Hint
Notes:

Website:
Email:
User Name:
Password:
Security Question/Hint
Notes:

Website:
Email:
User Name:
Password:
Security Question/Hint
Notes:

A

Website:
Email:
User Name:
Password:
Security Question/Hint
Notes:

Website:
Email:
User Name:
Password:
Security Question/Hint
Notes:

Website:
Email:
User Name:
Password:
Security Question/Hint
Notes:

A

Website:	
Email:	
User Name:	
Password:	
Security Question/Hint	
Notes:	

Website:	
Email:	
User Name:	
Password:	
Security Question/Hint	
Notes:	

Website:	
Email:	
User Name:	
Password:	
Security Question/Hint	
Notes:	

A

Website:
Email:
User Name:
Password:
Security Question/Hint
Notes:

Website:
Email:
User Name:
Password:
Security Question/Hint
Notes:

User Name:
Password:
Security Question/Hint
Notes:

Website:	
Email:	**B**
User Name:	
Password:	
Security Question/Hint	
Notes:	

Website:
Email:
User Name:
Password:
Security Question/Hint
Notes:

Website:
Email:
User Name:
Password:
Security Question/Hint
Notes:

B

Website:
Email:
User Name:
Password:
Security Question/Hint
Notes:

Website:
Email:
User Name:
Password:
Security Question/Hint
Notes:

Website:
Email:
User Name:
Password:
Security Question/Hint
Notes:

Website:
Email:
User Name:
Password:
Security Question/Hint
Notes:

Website:
Email:
User Name:
Password:
Security Question/Hint
Notes:

Website:
Email:
User Name:
Password:
Security Question/Hint
Notes:

B

Website:
Email:
User Name:
Password:
Security Question/Hint
Notes:

Website:
Email:
User Name:
Password:
Security Question/Hint
Notes:

Website:
Email:
User Name:
Password:
Security Question/Hint
Notes:

Website:
Email:
User Name:
Password:
Security Question/Hint
Notes:

C

Website:
Email:
User Name:
Password:
Security Question/Hint
Notes:

Website:
Email:
User Name:
Password:
Security Question/Hint
Notes:

C

Website:
Email:
User Name:
Password:
Security Question/Hint
Notes:

Website:
Email:
User Name:
Password:
Security Question/Hint
Notes:

Website:
Email:
User Name:
Password:
Security Question/Hint
Notes:

C

Website:
Email:
User Name:
Password:
Security Question/Hint
Notes:

Website:
Email:
User Name:
Password:
Security Question/Hint
Notes:

Website:
Email:
User Name:
Password:
Security Question/Hint
Notes:

C

| Website: |
| Email: |
| User Name: |
| Password: |
| |
| |
| Security Question/Hint |
| |
| Notes: |
| |

| Website: |
| Email: |
| User Name: |
| Password: |
| |
| |
| Security Question/Hint |
| |
| Notes: |
| |

| Website: |
| Email: |
| User Name: |
| Password: |
| |
| |
| Security Question/Hint |
| |
| Notes: |
| |

D

Website:
Email:
User Name:
Password:
Security Question/Hint
Notes:

Website:
Email:
User Name:
Password:
Security Question/Hint
Notes:

Website:
Email:
User Name:
Password:
Security Question/Hint
Notes:

D

Website:
Email:
User Name:
Password:
Security Question/Hint
Notes:

Website:
Email:
User Name:
Password:
Security Question/Hint
Notes:

Website:
Email:
User Name:
Password:
Security Question/Hint
Notes:

D

Website:
Email:
User Name:
Password:
Security Question/Hint
Notes:

Website:
Email:
User Name:
Password:
Security Question/Hint
Notes:

Website:
Email:
User Name:
Password:
Security Question/Hint
Notes:

D

Website:
Email:
User Name:
Password:
Security Question/Hint
Notes:

Website:
Email:
User Name:
Password:
Security Question/Hint
Notes:

Website:
Email:
User Name:
Password:
Security Question/Hint
Notes:

E

Website:
Email:
User Name:
Password:
Security Question/Hint
Notes:

Website:
Email:
User Name:
Password:
Security Question/Hint
Notes:

Website:
Email:
User Name:
Password:
Security Question/Hint
Notes:

E

| Website: |
| Email: |
| User Name: |
| Password: |
| |
| |
| Security Question/Hint |
| |
| Notes: |
| |

| Website: |
| Email: |
| User Name: |
| Password: |
| |
| |
| Security Question/Hint |
| |
| Notes: |
| |

| Website: |
| Email: |
| User Name: |
| Password: |
| |
| |
| Security Question/Hint |
| |
| Notes: |
| |

E

Website:
Email:
User Name:
Password:
Security Question/Hint
Notes:

Website:
Email:
User Name:
Password:
Security Question/Hint
Notes:

Website:
Email:
User Name:
Password:
Security Question/Hint
Notes:

| Website: |
| Email: |
| User Name: |
| Password: |
| |
| |
| Security Question/Hint |
| |
| Notes: |
| |

| Website: |
| Email: |
| User Name: |
| Password: |
| |
| |
| Security Question/Hint |
| |
| Notes: |
| |

| Website: |
| Email: |
| User Name: |
| Password: |
| |
| |
| Security Question/Hint |
| |
| Notes: |
| |

F

| Website: |
| Email: |
| User Name: |
| Password: |
| |
| |
| Security Question/Hint |
| |
| Notes: |
| |

| Website: |
| Email: |
| User Name: |
| Password: |
| |
| |
| Security Question/Hint |
| |
| Notes: |
| |

| Website: |
| Email: |
| User Name: |
| Password: |
| |
| |
| Security Question/Hint |
| |
| Notes: |
| |

F

Website:
Email:
User Name:
Password:
Security Question/Hint
Notes:

Website:
Email:
User Name:
Password:
Security Question/Hint
Notes:

Website:
Email:
User Name:
Password:
Security Question/Hint
Notes:

F

| Website: |
| Email: |
| User Name: |
| Password: |
| |
| |
| Security Question/Hint |
| |
| Notes: |
| |

| Website: |
| Email: |
| User Name: |
| Password: |
| |
| |
| Security Question/Hint |
| |
| Notes: |
| |

| Website: |
| Email: |
| User Name: |
| Password: |
| |
| |
| Security Question/Hint |
| |
| Notes: |
| |

F

Website:

Email:

User Name:

Password:

Security Question/Hint

Notes:

Website:

Email:

User Name:

Password:

Security Question/Hint

Notes:

Website:

Email:

User Name:

Password:

Security Question/Hint

Notes:

G

Website:
Email:
User Name:
Password:
Security Question/Hint
Notes:

Website:
Email:
User Name:
Password:
Security Question/Hint
Notes:

Website:
Email:
User Name:
Password:
Security Question/Hint
Notes:

G

Website:
Email:
User Name:
Password:
Security Question/Hint
Notes:

Website:
Email:
User Name:
Password:
Security Question/Hint
Notes:

Website:
Email:
User Name:
Password:
Security Question/Hint
Notes:

G

Website:
Email:
User Name:
Password:
Security Question/Hint
Notes:

Website:
Email:
User Name:
Password:
Security Question/Hint
Notes:

Website:
Email:
User Name:
Password:
Security Question/Hint
Notes:

G

| Website: |
| Email: |
| User Name: |
| Password: |
| |
| |
| Security Question/Hint |
| |
| Notes: |
| |

| Website: |
| Email: |
| User Name: |
| Password: |
| |
| |
| Security Question/Hint |
| |
| Notes: |
| |

| Website: |
| Email: |
| User Name: |
| Password: |
| |
| |
| Security Question/Hint |
| |
| Notes: |
| |

H

Website:	
Email:	
User Name:	
Password:	
Security Question/Hint	
Notes:	

Website:
Email:
User Name:
Password:
Security Question/Hint
Notes:

Website:
Email:
User Name:
Password:
Security Question/Hint
Notes:

Website:
Email:
User Name:
Password:
Security Question/Hint
Notes:

Website:
Email:
User Name:
Password:
Security Question/Hint
Notes:

Website:
Email:
User Name:
Password:
Security Question/Hint
Notes:

H

Website:
Email:
User Name:
Password:
Security Question/Hint
Notes:

Website:
Email:
User Name:
Password:
Security Question/Hint
Notes:

Website:
Email:
User Name:
Password:
Security Question/Hint
Notes:

H

Website:
Email:
User Name:
Password:
Security Question/Hint
Notes:

Website:
Email:
User Name:
Password:
Security Question/Hint
Notes:

Website:
Email:
User Name:
Password:
Security Question/Hint
Notes:

Website:	
Email:	
User Name:	
Password:	
Security Question/Hint	
Notes:	

I

Website:	
Email:	
User Name:	
Password:	
Security Question/Hint	
Notes:	

Website:	
Email:	
User Name:	
Password:	
Security Question/Hint	
Notes:	

I

Website:
Email:
User Name:
Password:
Security Question/Hint
Notes:

Website:
Email:
User Name:
Password:
Security Question/Hint
Notes:

Website:
Email:
User Name:
Password:
Security Question/Hint
Notes:

I

Website:
Email:
User Name:
Password:
Security Question/Hint
Notes:

Website:
Email:
User Name:
Password:
Security Question/Hint
Notes:

Website:
Email:
User Name:
Password:
Security Question/Hint
Notes:

I

Website:
Email:
User Name:
Password:
Security Question/Hint
Notes:

Website:
Email:
User Name:
Password:
Security Question/Hint
Notes:

Website:
Email:
User Name:
Password:
Security Question/Hint
Notes:

J

Website:
Email:
User Name:
Password:
Security Question/Hint
Notes:

Website:
Email:
User Name:
Password:
Security Question/Hint
Notes:

Website:
Email:
User Name:
Password:
Security Question/Hint
Notes:

J

Website:
Email:
User Name:
Password:
Security Question/Hint
Notes:

Website:
Email:
User Name:
Password:
Security Question/Hint
Notes:

Website:
Email:
User Name:
Password:
Security Question/Hint
Notes:

J

Website:
Email:
User Name:
Password:
Security Question/Hint
Notes:

Website:
Email:
User Name:
Password:
Security Question/Hint
Notes:

Website:
Email:
User Name:
Password:
Security Question/Hint
Notes:

J

Website:
Email:
User Name:
Password:
Security Question/Hint
Notes:

Website:
Email:
User Name:
Password:
Security Question/Hint
Notes:

Website:
Email:
User Name:
Password:
Security Question/Hint
Notes:

K

Website:
Email:
User Name:
Password:
Security Question/Hint
Notes:

Website:
Email:
User Name:
Password:
Security Question/Hint
Notes:

Website:
Email:
User Name:
Password:
Security Question/Hint
Notes:

K

Website:
Email:
User Name:
Password:
Security Question/Hint
Notes:

Website:
Email:
User Name:
Password:
Security Question/Hint
Notes:

Website:
Email:
User Name:
Password:
Security Question/Hint
Notes:

Website:	**K**
Email:	
User Name:	
Password:	
Security Question/Hint	
Notes:	

Website:
Email:
User Name:
Password:
Security Question/Hint
Notes:

Website:
Email:
User Name:
Password:
Security Question/Hint
Notes:

Website:
Email:
User Name:
Password:
Security Question/Hint
Notes:

Website:
Email:
User Name:
Password:
Security Question/Hint
Notes:

Website:
Email:
User Name:
Password:
Security Question/Hint
Notes:

L

Website:
Email:
User Name:
Password:
Security Question/Hint
Notes:

Website:
Email:
User Name:
Password:
Security Question/Hint
Notes:

Website:
Email:
User Name:
Password:
Security Question/Hint
Notes:

L

Website:
Email:
User Name:
Password:
Security Question/Hint
Notes:

Website:
Email:
User Name:
Password:
Security Question/Hint
Notes:

Website:
Email:
User Name:
Password:
Security Question/Hint
Notes:

L

Website:
Email:
User Name:
Password:
Security Question/Hint
Notes:

Website:
Email:
User Name:
Password:
Security Question/Hint
Notes:

Website:
Email:
User Name:
Password:
Security Question/Hint
Notes:

L

Website:
Email:
User Name:
Password:
Security Question/Hint
Notes:

Website:
Email:
User Name:
Password:
Security Question/Hint
Notes:

Website:
Email:
User Name:
Password:
Security Question/Hint
Notes:

M

Website:
Email:
User Name:
Password:
Security Question/Hint
Notes:

Website:
Email:
User Name:
Password:
Security Question/Hint
Notes:

Website:
Email:
User Name:
Password:
Security Question/Hint
Notes:

M

Website:
Email:
User Name:
Password:
Security Question/Hint
Notes:

Website:
Email:
User Name:
Password:
Security Question/Hint
Notes:

Website:
Email:
User Name:
Password:
Security Question/Hint
Notes:

Website:	**M**
Email:	
User Name:	
Password:	
Security Question/Hint	
Notes:	

Website:
Email:
User Name:
Password:
Security Question/Hint
Notes:

Website:
Email:
User Name:
Password:
Security Question/Hint
Notes:

M	Website:
	Email:
	User Name:
	Password:
	Security Question/Hint
	Notes:

Website:
Email:
User Name:
Password:
Security Question/Hint
Notes:

Website:
Email:
User Name:
Password:
Security Question/Hint
Notes:

Website:	
Email:	**N**
User Name:	
Password:	
Security Question/Hint	
Notes:	

Website:
Email:
User Name:
Password:
Security Question/Hint
Notes:

Website:
Email:
User Name:
Password:
Security Question/Hint
Notes:

N

Website:	
Email:	
User Name:	
Password:	
Security Question/Hint	
Notes:	

Website:	
Email:	
User Name:	
Password:	
Security Question/Hint	
Notes:	

Website:	
Email:	
User Name:	
Password:	
Security Question/Hint	
Notes:	

Website:
Email:
User Name:
Password:
Security Question/Hint
Notes:

Website:
Email:
User Name:
Password:
Security Question/Hint
Notes:

Website:
Email:
User Name:
Password:
Security Question/Hint
Notes:

N

Website:
Email:
User Name:
Password:
Security Question/Hint
Notes:

Website:
Email:
User Name:
Password:
Security Question/Hint
Notes:

Website:
Email:
User Name:
Password:
Security Question/Hint
Notes:

Website:
Email:
User Name:
Password:
Security Question/Hint
Notes:

O

Website:
Email:
User Name:
Password:
Security Question/Hint
Notes:

Website:
Email:
User Name:
Password:
Security Question/Hint
Notes:

O

| Website: |
| Email: |
| User Name: |
| Password: |
| |
| |
| Security Question/Hint |
| |
| Notes: |
| |

| Website: |
| Email: |
| User Name: |
| Password: |
| |
| |
| Security Question/Hint |
| |
| Notes: |
| |

| Website: |
| Email: |
| User Name: |
| Password: |
| |
| |
| Security Question/Hint |
| |
| Notes: |
| |

O

Website:
Email:
User Name:
Password:
Security Question/Hint
Notes:

Website:
Email:
User Name:
Password:
Security Question/Hint
Notes:

Website:
Email:
User Name:
Password:
Security Question/Hint
Notes:

O

Website:
Email:
User Name:
Password:
Security Question/Hint
Notes:

Website:
Email:
User Name:
Password:
Security Question/Hint
Notes:

Website:
Email:
User Name:
Password:
Security Question/Hint
Notes:

P

Website:
Email:
User Name:
Password:
Security Question/Hint
Notes:

Website:
Email:
User Name:
Password:
Security Question/Hint
Notes:

Website:
Email:
User Name:
Password:
Security Question/Hint
Notes:

P

Website:
Email:
User Name:
Password:
Security Question/Hint
Notes:

Website:
Email:
User Name:
Password:
Security Question/Hint
Notes:

Website:
Email:
User Name:
Password:
Security Question/Hint
Notes:

P

Website:
Email:
User Name:
Password:
Security Question/Hint
Notes:

Website:
Email:
User Name:
Password:
Security Question/Hint
Notes:

Website:
Email:
User Name:
Password:
Security Question/Hint
Notes:

P

Website:
Email:
User Name:
Password:
Security Question/Hint
Notes:

Website:
Email:
User Name:
Password:
Security Question/Hint
Notes:

Website:
Email:
User Name:
Password:
Security Question/Hint
Notes:

Q

Website:	
Email:	
User Name:	
Password:	
Security Question/Hint	
Notes:	

Website:	
Email:	
User Name:	
Password:	
Security Question/Hint	
Notes:	

Website:	
Email:	
User Name:	
Password:	
Security Question/Hint	
Notes:	

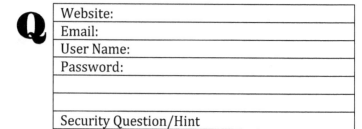

Website:

Email:

User Name:

Password:

Security Question/Hint

Notes:

Website:

Email:

User Name:

Password:

Security Question/Hint

Notes:

Website:

Email:

User Name:

Password:

Security Question/Hint

Notes:

Q

| Website: |
| Email: |
| User Name: |
| Password: |
| |
| |
| Security Question/Hint |
| |
| Notes: |
| |

| Website: |
| Email: |
| User Name: |
| Password: |
| |
| |
| Security Question/Hint |
| |
| Notes: |
| |

| Website: |
| Email: |
| User Name: |
| Password: |
| |
| |
| Security Question/Hint |
| |
| Notes: |
| |

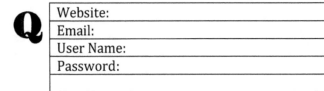

Website:
Email:
User Name:
Password:
Security Question/Hint
Notes:

Website:
Email:
User Name:
Password:
Security Question/Hint
Notes:

Website:
Email:
User Name:
Password:
Security Question/Hint
Notes:

R

Website:
Email:
User Name:
Password:
Security Question/Hint
Notes:

Website:
Email:
User Name:
Password:
Security Question/Hint
Notes:

Website:
Email:
User Name:
Password:
Security Question/Hint
Notes:

R

Website:
Email:
User Name:
Password:
Security Question/Hint
Notes:

Website:
Email:
User Name:
Password:
Security Question/Hint
Notes:

Website:
Email:
User Name:
Password:
Security Question/Hint
Notes:

Website:	**R**
Email:	
User Name:	
Password:	
Security Question/Hint	
Notes:	

Website:
Email:
User Name:
Password:
Security Question/Hint
Notes:

Website:
Email:
User Name:
Password:
Security Question/Hint
Notes:

Website:
Email:
User Name:
Password:
Security Question/Hint
Notes:

Website:
Email:
User Name:
Password:
Security Question/Hint
Notes:

Website:
Email:
User Name:
Password:
Security Question/Hint
Notes:

S

Website:
Email:
User Name:
Password:
Security Question/Hint
Notes:

Website:
Email:
User Name:
Password:
Security Question/Hint
Notes:

Website:
Email:
User Name:
Password:
Security Question/Hint
Notes:

S

Website:
Email:
User Name:
Password:
Security Question/Hint
Notes:

Website:
Email:
User Name:
Password:
Security Question/Hint
Notes:

Website:
Email:
User Name:
Password:
Security Question/Hint
Notes:

S

Website:
Email:
User Name:
Password:
Security Question/Hint
Notes:

Website:
Email:
User Name:
Password:
Security Question/Hint
Notes:

Website:
Email:
User Name:
Password:
Security Question/Hint
Notes:

S

Website:
Email:
User Name:
Password:
Security Question/Hint
Notes:

Website:
Email:
User Name:
Password:
Security Question/Hint
Notes:

Website:
Email:
User Name:
Password:
Security Question/Hint
Notes:

Website:	**T**
Email:	
User Name:	
Password:	
Security Question/Hint	
Notes:	

Website:
Email:
User Name:
Password:
Security Question/Hint
Notes:

Website:
Email:
User Name:
Password:
Security Question/Hint
Notes:

Website:
Email:
User Name:
Password:
Security Question/Hint
Notes:

Website:
Email:
User Name:
Password:
Security Question/Hint
Notes:

Website:
Email:
User Name:
Password:
Security Question/Hint
Notes:

Website:

Email:

User Name:

Password:

Security Question/Hint

Notes:

Website:

Email:

User Name:

Password:

Security Question/Hint

Notes:

Website:

Email:

User Name:

Password:

Security Question/Hint

Notes:

T

Website:
Email:
User Name:
Password:
Security Question/Hint
Notes:

Website:
Email:
User Name:
Password:
Security Question/Hint
Notes:

Website:
Email:
User Name:
Password:
Security Question/Hint
Notes:

U

Website:
Email:
User Name:
Password:
Security Question/Hint
Notes:

Website:
Email:
User Name:
Password:
Security Question/Hint
Notes:

Website:
Email:
User Name:
Password:
Security Question/Hint
Notes:

U

Website:
Email:
User Name:
Password:
Security Question/Hint
Notes:

Website:
Email:
User Name:
Password:
Security Question/Hint
Notes:

Website:
Email:
User Name:
Password:
Security Question/Hint
Notes:

U

Website:
Email:
User Name:
Password:
Security Question/Hint
Notes:

Website:
Email:
User Name:
Password:
Security Question/Hint
Notes:

Website:
Email:
User Name:
Password:
Security Question/Hint
Notes:

U

Website:
Email:
User Name:
Password:
Security Question/Hint
Notes:

Website:
Email:
User Name:
Password:
Security Question/Hint
Notes:

Website:
Email:
User Name:
Password:
Security Question/Hint
Notes:

V

Website:

Email:

User Name:

Password:

Security Question/Hint

Notes:

Website:

Email:

User Name:

Password:

Security Question/Hint

Notes:

Website:

Email:

User Name:

Password:

Security Question/Hint

Notes:

V

Website:
Email:
User Name:
Password:
Security Question/Hint
Notes:

Website:
Email:
User Name:
Password:
Security Question/Hint
Notes:

Website:
Email:
User Name:
Password:
Security Question/Hint
Notes:

V

Website:
Email:
User Name:
Password:
Security Question/Hint
Notes:

Website:
Email:
User Name:
Password:
Security Question/Hint
Notes:

Website:
Email:
User Name:
Password:
Security Question/Hint
Notes:

V

| Website: |
| Email: |
| User Name: |
| Password: |
| |
| |
| Security Question/Hint |
| |
| Notes: |
| |

| Website: |
| Email: |
| User Name: |
| Password: |
| |
| |
| Security Question/Hint |
| |
| Notes: |
| |

| Website: |
| Email: |
| User Name: |
| Password: |
| |
| |
| Security Question/Hint |
| |
| Notes: |
| |

Website:	**W**
Email:	
User Name:	
Password:	
Security Question/Hint	
Notes:	

Website:
Email:
User Name:
Password:
Security Question/Hint
Notes:

Website:
Email:
User Name:
Password:
Security Question/Hint
Notes:

Website:
Email:
User Name:
Password:
Security Question/Hint
Notes:

Website:
Email:
User Name:
Password:
Security Question/Hint
Notes:

Website:
Email:
User Name:
Password:
Security Question/Hint
Notes:

Website:	**W**
Email:	
User Name:	
Password:	
Security Question/Hint	
Notes:	

Website:
Email:
User Name:
Password:
Security Question/Hint
Notes:

Website:
Email:
User Name:
Password:
Security Question/Hint
Notes:

Website:
Email:
User Name:
Password:
Security Question/Hint
Notes:

Website:
Email:
User Name:
Password:
Security Question/Hint
Notes:

Website:
Email:
User Name:
Password:
Security Question/Hint
Notes:

X

Website:
Email:
User Name:
Password:
Security Question/Hint
Notes:

Website:
Email:
User Name:
Password:
Security Question/Hint
Notes:

Website:
Email:
User Name:
Password:
Security Question/Hint
Notes:

X

Website:
Email:
User Name:
Password:
Security Question/Hint
Notes:

Website:
Email:
User Name:
Password:
Security Question/Hint
Notes:

Website:
Email:
User Name:
Password:
Security Question/Hint
Notes:

X

Website:
Email:
User Name:
Password:
Security Question/Hint
Notes:

Website:
Email:
User Name:
Password:
Security Question/Hint
Notes:

Website:
Email:
User Name:
Password:
Security Question/Hint
Notes:

Website:
Email:
User Name:
Password:
Security Question/Hint
Notes:

Website:
Email:
User Name:
Password:
Security Question/Hint
Notes:

Website:
Email:
User Name:
Password:
Security Question/Hint
Notes:

Y

Website:
Email:
User Name:
Password:
Security Question/Hint
Notes:

Website:
Email:
User Name:
Password:
Security Question/Hint
Notes:

Website:
Email:
User Name:
Password:
Security Question/Hint
Notes:

Y

Website:
Email:
User Name:
Password:
Security Question/Hint
Notes:

Website:
Email:
User Name:
Password:
Security Question/Hint
Notes:

Website:
Email:
User Name:
Password:
Security Question/Hint
Notes:

Y

Website:
Email:
User Name:
Password:
Security Question/Hint
Notes:

Website:
Email:
User Name:
Password:
Security Question/Hint
Notes:

Website:
Email:
User Name:
Password:
Security Question/Hint
Notes:

Y

Website:
Email:
User Name:
Password:
Security Question/Hint
Notes:

Website:
Email:
User Name:
Password:
Security Question/Hint
Notes:

Website:
Email:
User Name:
Password:
Security Question/Hint
Notes:

Z

Website:
Email:
User Name:
Password:
Security Question/Hint
Notes:

Website:
Email:
User Name:
Password:
Security Question/Hint
Notes:

Website:
Email:
User Name:
Password:
Security Question/Hint
Notes:

Website:
Email:
User Name:
Password:
Security Question/Hint
Notes:

Website:
Email:
User Name:
Password:
Security Question/Hint
Notes:

Website:
Email:
User Name:
Password:
Security Question/Hint
Notes:

Z

Website:

Email:

User Name:

Password:

Security Question/Hint

Notes:

Website:

Email:

User Name:

Password:

Security Question/Hint

Notes:

Website:

Email:

User Name:

Password:

Security Question/Hint

Notes:

Website:
Email:
User Name:
Password:
Security Question/Hint
Notes:

Website:
Email:
User Name:
Password:
Security Question/Hint
Notes:

Website:
Email:
User Name:
Password:
Security Question/Hint
Notes:

≪ NOTES ≫

NOTES

www.ingramcontent.com/pod-product-compliance
Lightning Source LLC
Chambersburg PA
CBHW070842070326
40690CB00009B/1653